D1523282

Deep Space Discovery

PLUTO
AND OTHER DWARF PLANETS

GAIL TERP

WORLD BOOK

This World Book edition of *Pluto and Other Dwarf Planets* is published by agreement between Black Rabbit Books and World Book, Inc.
© 2019 Black Rabbit Books,
2140 Howard Dr. West,
North Mankato, MN 56003 U.S.A.
World Book, Inc.,
180 North LaSalle St., Suite 900,
Chicago, IL 60601 U.S.A.

Marysa Storm, editor; Grant Gould, designer; Omay Ayres, photo researcher

Library of Congress Control Number: 2017023680

ISBN: 978-0-7166-3465-2

Printed in China. 3/18

BOLT

Image Credits

Alamy: Irina Dmitrienko, Cover (Pluto); dawn.jpl.nasa.gov: JPL/NASA, 26–27; fr.wikipedia.org: NASA, 18 (Haumea); hdwallsbox.com: skydiverlab.com, 8–9; nasa.gov: NASA, 14–15, 28–29 (New Horizons); Science Source: Detlev van Ravenswaay, 18 (bkgd); John R. Foster, 12 (bkgd); Mark Garlick, 17; Mikkel Juul Jensen, 10–11; Spencer Sutton, 20 (dwarf planets), 22–23; Shutterstock: Aphelleon, 23; Azuzl, 20 (bttm l dwarf planets); HelenField, 1, 24; jaroslava V, 32; John T Takai, 7; Jurik Peter, 6 (bttm); mozzyb, 3; Natykach Nataliia, 31; notbad, 12 (weights); Oleksandrum, 6 (top); smartdesign91, 18 (arrows); Vadim Sadovski, 4–5, 28–29 (space); Yuriy Mazur, 20 (lower l bkgd); solarsystem.nasa.gov/: NASA, Cover (New Horizons)
Every effort has been made to contact copyright holders for material reproduced in this book. Any omissions will be rectified in subsequent printings if notice is given to the publisher.

CONTENTS

In 1929, a young man began working for an **observatory**. His name was Clyde Tombaugh. His job was to find a new planet. He studied pictures of the night sky for a year. Then, in 1930, he made a big discovery. He found a tiny speck that moved through the sky like a planet. He discovered what came to be called Pluto.

The Three Rules for Planets

RULE ONE
It must **orbit** a star.

RULE TWO
It must be mostly round.

RULE THREE
Its path must be clear of smaller objects.

Defining Planets

For 76 years, people called Pluto a planet. Then, in 2006, that changed. Scientists had found other bodies in space similar to Pluto. Some of them were even larger than Pluto. Scientists didn't feel they should all be planets. So they made three rules for planets. Objects that only follow the first two rules, such as Pluto, would be dwarf planets.

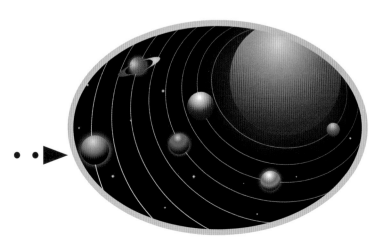

Their Place in Space

The sun is the center of Earth's solar system. Eight planets and many dwarf planets circle around it. The sun's **gravity** keeps them all in their orbits.

Dwarf planets are found in the Kuiper and main asteroid belts. The Kuiper Belt lies past Neptune. The main asteroid belt is between Mars and Jupiter.

The Kuiper Belt is a band of icy bodies and **comets**. Thousands of asteroids make up the main asteroid belt.

DWARF PLANETS AND THE SOLAR SYSTEM

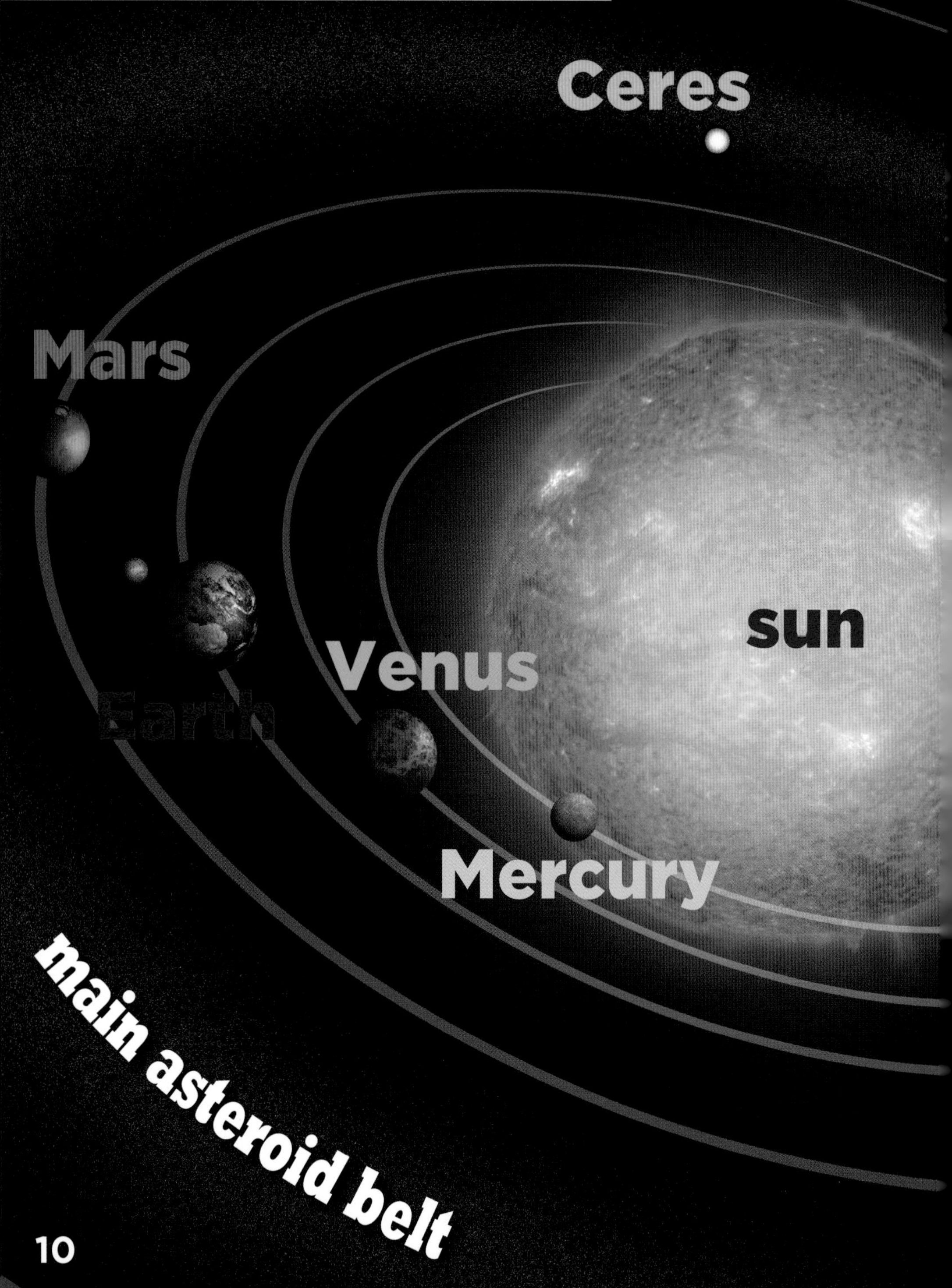

Ceres

Mars

sun

Venus

Earth

Mercury

main asteroid belt

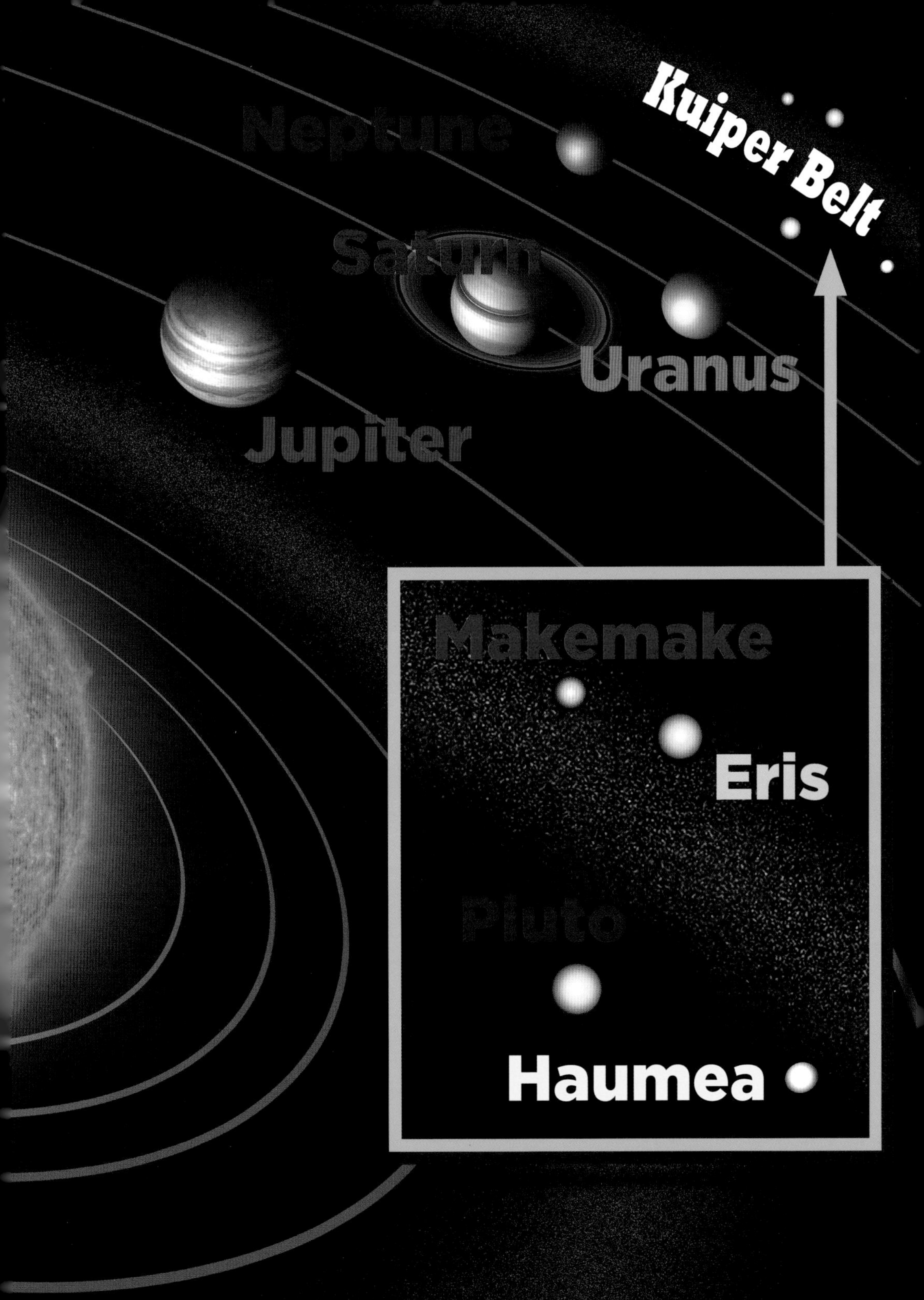

Neptune

Saturn

Jupiter

Uranus

Makemake

Eris

Pluto

Haumea

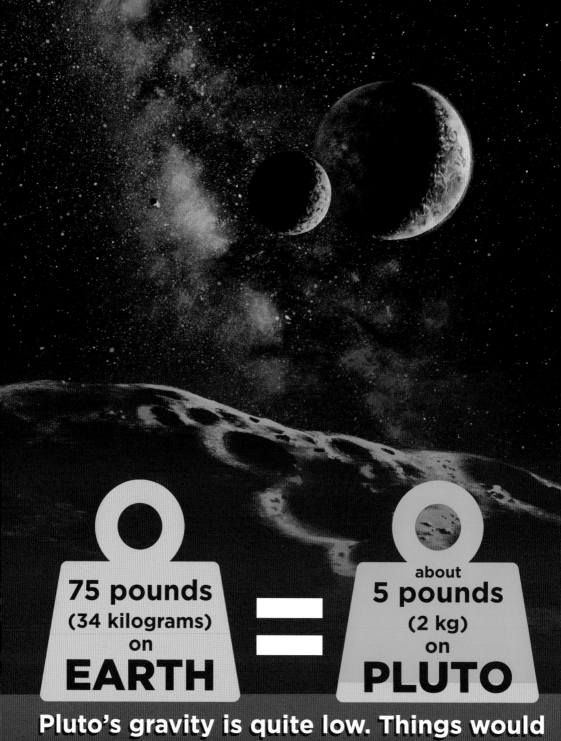

75 pounds
(34 kilograms)
on
EARTH

=

about
5 pounds
(2 kg)
on
PLUTO

Pluto's gravity is quite low. Things would weigh less on Pluto than they do on Earth.

CHAPTER 2

A CLOSER LOOK at Pluto

Pluto is the most well-known dwarf planet. The dwarf planet is found in the Kuiper Belt. At its farthest, Pluto is 4.67 billion miles (7.5 billion kilometers) from Earth.

Pluto is covered with frozen gas. It also has **craters** and mountains. Five moons orbit Pluto.

Pluto

DIAMETER
about
1,470 MILES
(2,366 km)

AVERAGE DISTANCE
FROM THE SUN
**3.67 billion miles
(5.9 billion km)**

AVERAGE SURFACE TEMPERATURE
**-387 to -369 degrees
Fahrenheit**
(-233 to -223 degrees Celsius)

Earth

AVERAGE DISTANCE FROM THE SUN
93 million miles
(150 million km)

AVERAGE SURFACE TEMPERATURE
60 degrees Fahrenheit
(16 degrees C)

DIAMETER
7,926 MILES
(12,756 km) at equator

CHAPTER 3

OTHER Dwarf Planets

Pluto is one of the first five confirmed dwarf planets. The other four are Ceres, Eris, Haumea, and Makemake.

Ceres is in the main asteroid belt. It was discovered in 1801. It's covered with many small craters.

Eris is in the Kuiper Belt. It was first seen in 2003. Like Pluto, ice covers its surface. The ice makes it look shiny. One moon orbits Eris.

Number of Moons

				5	5
					4
					3
			2		2
	1	1			1
0					0
Ceres	Eris	Makemake	Haumea	Pluto	

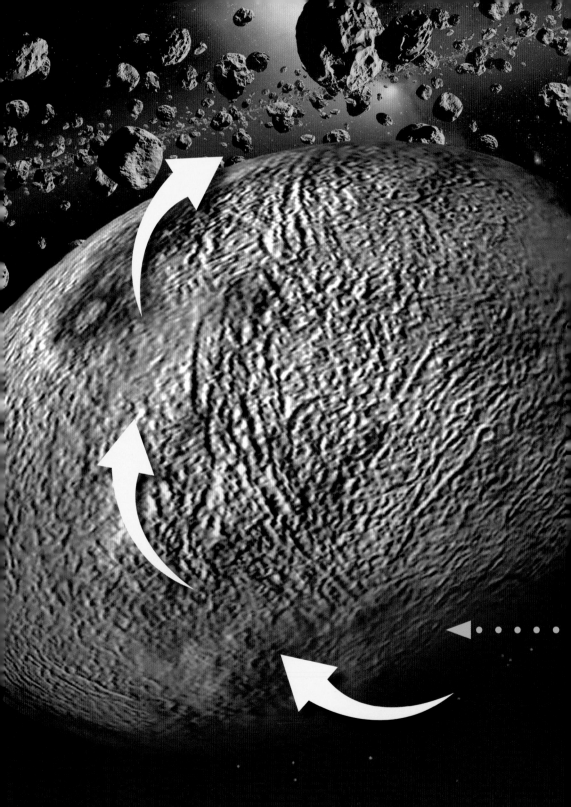

Haumea and Makemake

Haumea orbits in the Kuiper Belt. It is not round. Instead, it's shaped more like a football. Haumea's shape comes from how quickly it spins.

Also in the Kuiper Belt is Makemake. **Astronomers** discovered it in 2005. Frozen gas covers its surface. The gas may be the source of Makemake's reddish color.

Haumea is one of the fastest spinning objects in space. It spins around once every four hours. That means its days are only four hours long.

Diameter

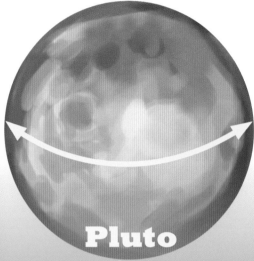

Pluto
about
1,470 miles
(2,366 km)

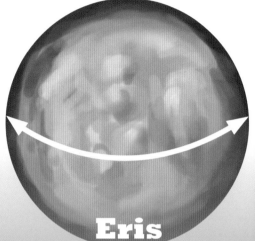

Eris
about
1,450 miles
(2,334 km)

HOW LONG IT TAKES TO ORBIT THE SUN

Haumea
285 Earth years

Eris
557 Earth years

Makemake
310 Earth years

Pluto
248 Earth years

Ceres
5 Earth years

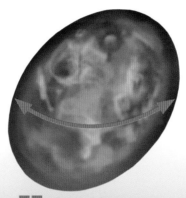

Makemake
about
900 miles
(1,448 km)

Haumea
up to
1,218 miles
(1,960 km)

Ceres
up to
605 miles
(974 km)

Length of Day

Pluto	**153** Earth hours
Eris	**26** Earth hours
Makemake	**22.5** Earth hours
Ceres	**9** Earth hours
Haumea	**4** Earth hours

CHAPTER 4

Dwarf Planet

In 2006, a **probe** called *New Horizons* left Earth. Its mission was to study Pluto. In 2015, it finally reached the dwarf planet. From space, it studied Pluto's surface. It collected data about its moons.

Pluto
Discovery

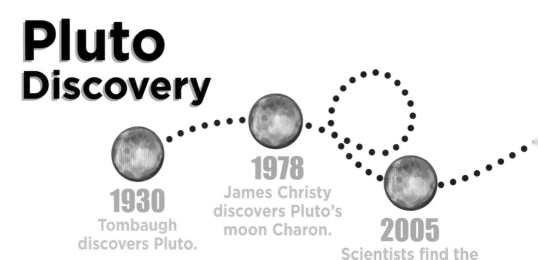

1930
Tombaugh discovers Pluto.

1978
James Christy discovers Pluto's moon Charon.

2005
Scientists find the moons Nix and Hydra.

2006
Pluto becomes
a dwarf planet.
NASA launches
New Horizons.

2011
Mark Showalter
discovers
the moon
Kerberos.

2012
Showalter finds
the moon Styx.

2015
New Horizons
reaches Pluto.

More to Explore

• • • • • • *New Horizons'* work isn't done. It'll stay in the Kuiper Belt. In 2019, it should reach an icy body far past Pluto. *New Horizons* will study the **ancient** object. Scientists will use the data to learn more about the solar system.

Some scientists believe there may be more than 100 dwarf planets.

Exploring Other Dwarf Planets

Pluto isn't the only dwarf planet spacecraft have visited. The spacecraft *Dawn* currently studies Ceres. *Dawn* takes photos of the dwarf planet. It also searches for water ice beneath Ceres' surface.

Spectacular Space

Scientists have learned a lot about dwarf planets over the years. But there is much more to learn.

Studying dwarf planets can help scientists learn more about the solar system. The research tells people about its history and humans' place in it.

ancient (AYN-shunt)—from a time long ago

astronomer (uh-STRON-uh-mer)—an expert in the science of heavenly bodies and of their sizes, motions, and composition

comet (KOM-it)—an icy rock in outer space that develops a long, bright tail when it passes near the sun

crater (KREY-ter)—a hole formed by an impact

equator (ih-KWEY-ter)—an imaginary circle around Earth that is equally distant from the North Pole and the South Pole

gravity (GRAV-i-tee)—the natural force that pulls physical things toward each other

observatory (uhb-ZUR-vuh-tawr-ee)—a special building for studying stars, planets, and weather

orbit (AWR-bit)—the path taken by one body circling around another body

probe (prohb)—a device used to collect information from outer space and send it back to Earth

BOOKS

Carson, Mary Kay. *Mission to Pluto: The First Visit to an Ice Dwarf and the Kuiper Belt.* Scientists in the Field. Boston: Houghton Mifflin Harcourt, 2016.

Roland, James. *Pluto: A Space Discovery Guide.* Space Discovery Guides. Minneapolis: Lerner Publications, 2017.

Saxena, Shalini. *Pluto and Other Dwarf Planets.* Planetary Exploration. New York: Britannica Educational Publishing in association with Rosen Educational Services, 2017.

WEBSITES

Dwarf Planets
kids.nationalgeographic.com/explore/space/dwarf-planets/#dwarf-planet-red.jpg

Peculiar Pluto
spaceplace.nasa.gov/ice-dwarf/en/

Planets and Moons
www.esa.int/esaKIDSen/SEM8BTMZCIE_OurUniverse_0.html

INDEX